THE Love

FIFTEEN STORIES & ESSAYS

Editor: John Langan
Introduction by Beth Johnson

 TP THE TOWNSEND LIBRARY

THE POWER OF LOVE

Ubi caritas est vera, Deus ibi est.
(Wherever love is true, God is there.)

TP **THE TOWNSEND LIBRARY**

For more titles in the Townsend Library,
visit our website: **www.townsendpress.com**

Copyright © 2015 by Townsend Press, Inc.
Printed in the United States of America

10 9 8 7 6 5 4 3 2 1

Cover and illustrations © 2015 by Hal Taylor

All rights reserved. Any **one** chapter
of this book may be reproduced without
the written permission of the publisher.
For permission to reproduce more than
one chapter, send requests to:

Townsend Press, Inc.
439 Kelley Drive
West Berlin, NJ 08091
permissions@townsendpress.com

ISBN-13: 978-1-59194-456-0

Library of Congress Control Number:
2014953581

CONTENTS

what did he say about
her?
Was she talking about
him too?

INTRODUCTION

Is there any word in the English language that is tossed around more casually than "love"?

We love our cars. We love pizza. We love our iPhones, our favorite drinks and movies and songs and TV shows of the moment. Our playlists are stuffed with songs about love—from classics like the Beatles "Love Me Do" to Rihanna's "We Found Love." "Love" is the operative word in commercials for everything from hamburgers (McDonald's "I'm lovin' it") to beauty products (Olay's "Love the skin you're in.")

Love, love, love.

With that kind of "love" all around us, it's sometimes easy to forget the truly profound nature of love. Love is a fundamental force. Not unlike gravity, it exerts its pull in ways that are both irresistible and hard to understand. We can't always put our love into words, or explain how it works. We just know it's there. It moves us deeply. It changes things.

Fortunately, when we are stunned by love's power and stand wordless and amazed, we have the poets to speak for us. One of the most beautiful expressions of love ever written comes to us from William Shakespeare. His Sonnet 116 begins with these famous lines:

> *Let me not to the marriage of true minds*
> *Admit impediments.*
> *Love is not love*
> *Which alters when it alteration finds . . .*

A modern take on Shakespeare's language might
be this:

> *Let me not declare any reasons why two*
> *True-minded people should not be married.*
> *Love is not love*
> *Which changes when it finds a change in*
>   *circumstances . . .*

While Shakespeare is commenting on love that
leads to marriage, his words apply to any love
that is deep and true. Love does not change
when the unexpected happens. Love knows that
life is filled with uncertainty, and it stands firm in
the face of misfortune.

A beautiful illustration of love that does not
"alter when it alteration finds" appears in the
book *About Alice*, in which author Calvin Trillin
remembers his wife, who had died not long
before. He describes a time that Alice volunteered
at a camp for children with disabilities. Alice
had become especially close to a little girl she
called by her initial, L. The child had genetic
diseases that kept her from growing normally and
from digesting food. She had difficulty walking.
She had to be fed through a tube at night.
Still, the little girl was, in Alice's words, "the
most optimistic, most enthusiastic, most hopeful

human being I had ever encountered."

As Alice grew closer to the little girl, she became more curious about L. What had given her, despite her many challenges, such joy and optimism? What was her secret?

Then one day at camp, while the children were playing a game, L. asked Alice to hold her mail. On top of the pile was a note from L.'s mother. Alice glanced at it and saw the words that L.'s mother had written to her daughter. They read, "If God had given us all the children in the world to choose from, L., we would only have chosen you."

Love is not love / which alters when it alteration finds. L.'s mother loved her physically challenged, "different" daughter exactly as she was. That unshakeable love shone through L., giving her the radiant strength and optimism that so impressed Alice.

That kind of love, powerful and mysterious, is the subject of this collection of true stories. You will read about a parent's love for a child, and children's for their parents. There are stories about strangers thrown together who form a bond that can only be called love. You'll find love involving the young and the old, the single and the coupled, and even the non-human and their people. There is the love that leads to marriage, the love of lasting friendships, and the love of a cause that is right and noble.

Throughout them all, you will witness the

kind of love that Shakespeare describes when he writes, later in Sonnet 116:

> *Love's not Time's fool, though rosy lips and*
> > *cheeks*
> *Within his bending sickle's compass come.*
> *Love alters not with his brief hours and weeks,*
> *But bears it out even to the edge of doom.*
> *If this be error and upon me proved,*
> *I never writ, nor no man ever loved.*

Today's version might say:

> *Love is not at the mercy of Time, though*
> > *physical beauty*
> *Is mowed down by his blade.*
> *Love does not alter within hours and weeks,*
> *But, rather, it endures until the last day*
> > *of life.*
> *If I am proved wrong about these thoughts*
> > *on love,*
> *Then I never wrote a word, and no man has*
> > *ever loved.*

As you read through this collection, consider the thread that runs through it: the idea that love—not the "love" that we read about on billboards or toss about in casual conversation—is a fundamental force; one that makes people capable of becoming better and stronger, braver and more generous, than they ever knew possible. May these stories of love that "does not alter when it alteration finds" inspire you to consider the incredible power of love.

The Blind Vet

Preview

A flash of light, an explosion—and a young man would never see again. Nick came home from the war scared, angry, and depressed. Would his life ever seem worthwhile again? That question was answered by the love of one special person.

The Blind Vet

Tanya Savory

When Nick boarded the bus, everyone looked at him. A few people shook their heads in pity. It didn't seem right that such a young man should have so much trouble climbing the three short steps up to the bus aisle.

"Why does that man have that white stick?" a small girl asked her mother loudly.

"Shh!" the mother said quickly. "It's not polite to talk about him, honey. He's blind."

But Nick had heard the little girl. In fact, he could feel everyone's eyes on him even though he couldn't see them. Using his cane, Nick carefully measured the height of each step. Gripping the handrail with white knuckles, he slowly made his way to the aisle. Then he used his hands to feel his way. Gratefully, Nick eased into the first set of seats reserved for the disabled. A thin rivulet of sweat trickled down Nick's forehead, and his hands shook.

Okay. Relax. Nick tried to calm himself down. *You'll be all right. You'll make it.*

Nick, barely 22, had been blind for just over a year. During a tour of duty in Afghanistan, the vehicle Nick had been riding in had run over an IED. Nick remembered a bright flash, a terrible explosion, and the screams of his comrades. Then, the bright color of his own blood in his eyes was the last thing Nick ever saw. Fragments of metal and glass had scarred his face and destroyed his eyes.

When he came home from the war, Nick was frightened. What would his friends think of him? Two of Nick's favorite pastimes had been cycling and playing basketball, and that's how he had met a lot of his friends. Now he wouldn't be able to do either. Would his friends even want to be around him anymore?

But Nick's biggest apprehension was that his girlfriend, Kristen, would leave him. The two of them had been together since high school, and Nick had secretly planned on proposing to Kristen when he returned from Afghanistan. But he never dreamed that he'd be returning like this. Now Kristen would have to take care of him—if she even wanted to stay with him. *And why would she want to stay with him*, Nick wondered. Kristen was funny and smart. Plus, she was beautiful with long red hair and bright green eyes. *She won't want to waste her time with some blind guy who can't even see her*, Nick thought bitterly. *She'll never marry me now.*

At first, Nick's friends came around a lot. They

sat and talked with him, trying to get him to laugh at old jokes. They brought him foods he liked and often hung around for hours listening to music or reading the newspaper to Nick. They rarely mentioned basketball or the upcoming cycling races they were training for—they thought this would make Nick sad. In fact, they rarely even mentioned Nick's blindness because it made them uncomfortable. And, in time, most of Nick's friends' discomfort with his blindness outweighed their concern for him. They ran out of things to talk about. One by one, most of Nick's friends faded away.

Now Nick became angry and depressed. He felt betrayed and abandoned by friends, and he declined into self-pity. Nick might have sunk all the way to rock bottom if it had not been for Kristen. During that very difficult first year, Kristen never wavered in her devotion to Nick. She helped him in any way she could, even when Nick's frustration made it hard for her to help him.

"I'm blind!" he'd sometimes shout angrily. "Why are you ruining your life by staying with me? I'm no good anymore. Why don't you go find someone who can *see* you—someone who doesn't have to be treated like a baby?"

More than anything, Nick hated his loss of independence. He'd always prided himself on the fact that he was never afraid to try new things and go to new places. Sometimes on long weekend bike rides, Nick would make himself get lost intentionally just to see what kind of adventure it might turn into. Now he couldn't even walk to the corner store without Kristen's help.

Kristen knew that Nick needed to feel some sense of independence, or he would only become angrier and sadder. As it was, he often spent entire days doing little more than listening to the radio, sleeping, and drinking beer—something he'd rarely done before. So when Kristen came across an article about a local center for disabled veterans, she mentioned it to Nick.

"It's a way for you to meet other men and women like yourself," Kristen explained. "And there's all kinds of help there to get you trained and prepared for a new career."

"Career?" Nick asked doubtfully. "What could I do without my eyes?"

Kristen walked over and took Nick's hands in hers. "A lot, Nick," she said quietly. "Why don't you go and find out?"

Nick agreed to give it a try. There was only one catch. The center didn't open until 9:00, and since Kristen had to be at work at 8:30, she would not be able to drive Nick there every day.

"Nick, the city bus stops right in front of the center," Kristen said carefully. "Why don't you learn how to take the bus?"

"Take the bus?" Nick replied angrily. "How would I even know where I was going? What if I get lost? I feel like you're abandoning me—just like all my friends did."

Kristen thought Nick might respond like this, so she had already figured out a plan. "Look," she said, "I'll make some arrangements at work. I'll ride the bus with you for a week or so until you get the hang of it. What do you think of that?"

It took a little more convincing, but Nick finally decided to try. And, actually, he was excited about the idea of something new—something he could do on his own.

And so, for a week and a half, Nick and Kristen took the bus together across town. She helped him use his cane to feel for the curb, the bus steps, and the aisle to his seat. They counted the number of stops it took to get from their apartment to the center, and when they arrived, Kristen helped Nick find the sidewalk that led to the center's front door. If Nick stumbled or became confused, Kristen was there to smooth things over and encourage her boyfriend along.

Finally, Nick felt sufficiently confident to ride the bus alone. He'd been enjoying the time spent at the center, and he was looking forward to being independent again. But now as Nick sat on the bus alone for the first time, he wasn't so sure. He heard the little girl ask her mother again what was wrong with the man with the funny cane. Nick took a deep breath and tried to concentrate.

Two, three, four . . . Nick counted the stops. Very carefully, he got off at the seventh stop. Just like every day with Kristen, Nick used his cane to walk over the curb and to the sidewalk to the center. His heart was pounding. What if he was going the wrong way? What if he fell? No one was there to help him.

"Hey, Nick! Good to see you." Relief flooded

Nick. It was one of the instructors at the center. He'd made it!

At the end of his first week of riding alone, Nick was hardly nervous at all. Every day had gone well. Only one time had he tripped on the curb, but almost instantly the hand of a stranger had gripped his shoulder to keep him from falling. Nick had said thank you, but the stranger just patted him on the back.

Now as Nick carefully made his way down the steps of the bus, the bus driver said, "You sure are one lucky young man."

At first, Nick wasn't sure if the bus driver was talking to him. Why would anyone think he was lucky? "Me?" Nick asked.

"Yes, you!" the driver said with a friendly laugh.

"Why do you say that?"

"Well, to have someone looking out for you like that," the driver explained. "Making sure you're okay."

"What are you talking about?" Nick asked.

"You know," the driver said, sounding a little puzzled by Nick's question. "That pretty woman with the red hair—the one who has been standing on the corner waiting and watching for you every day this week. The one who caught you when you almost fell."

Nick was too stunned to say anything at first. Then tears filled his eyes behind his dark glasses.

The driver chuckled again and said, "I wish my wife cared that much about me!"

Nick smiled through his tears. "She's not my wife," he said quietly. "But she's going to be."

■ ■ ■

All the Good Things

Preview

One Friday afternoon, in one ninth-grade math class, a teacher's unplanned activity changed her students' mood from sullen to smiling. It would be years before she learned the lasting impact of her act of kindness.

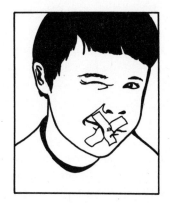

All the Good Things

Sister Helen Mrosla

He was in the first third-grade class I taught at Saint Mary's School in Morris, Minnesota. All thirty-four of my students were dear to me, but Mark Eklund was one in a million. He was very neat in appearance but had that happy-to-be-alive attitude that made even his occasional mischievousness delightful.

Mark talked incessantly. I had to remind him again and again that talking without permission was not acceptable. What impressed me so much, though, was his sincere response every time I had to correct him for misbehaving—"Thank you for correcting me, Sister!" I didn't know what to make of it at first, but before long I became accustomed to hearing it many times a day.

One morning my patience was growing thin when Mark talked once too often, and then I made a novice teacher's mistake. I looked at him and said, "If you say one more word, I am going to tape your mouth shut!"

It wasn't ten seconds later when Chuck blurted out, "Mark is talking again." I hadn't asked any of the students to help me watch Mark, but since I had stated the punishment in front of the class, I had to act on it.

I remember the scene as if it had occurred this morning. I walked to my desk, very deliberately opened my drawer, and took out a roll of masking tape. Without saying a word, I proceeded to Mark's desk, tore off two pieces of tape, and made a big X with them over his mouth. I then returned to the front of the room. As I glanced at Mark to see how he was doing, he winked at me.

That did it! I started laughing. The class cheered as I walked back to Mark's desk, removed the tape, and shrugged my shoulders. His first words were, "Thank you for correcting me, Sister."

At the end of the year I was asked to teach junior-high math. The years flew by, and before I knew it, Mark was in my classroom again. He was more handsome than ever and just as polite. Since he had to listen carefully to my instruction in the "new math," he did not talk as much in ninth grade as he had talked in the third.

One Friday, things just didn't feel right. We had worked hard on a new concept all week, and I sensed that the students were frowning, frustrated with themselves—and edgy with one another. I had to stop this crankiness before it got out of hand. So I asked them to list the names of the other students in the room on two sheets of paper, leaving a space after each name. Then I told them to think of the nicest thing they could say about each of their classmates and write it down.

It took the remainder of the class period to finish the assignment, and as the students left the room, each one handed me the papers. Charlie smiled. Mark said, "Thank you for teaching me, Sister. Have a good weekend."

That Saturday, I wrote down the name of each student on a separate sheet of paper, and I listed what everyone else had said about that individual.

On Monday I gave each student his or her list. Before long, the entire class was smiling. "Really?" I heard whispered. "I never knew that meant anything to anyone!" "I didn't know others liked me so much!"

No one ever mentioned those papers in class again. I never knew if the students discussed them after class or with their parents, but it didn't matter. The exercise had accomplished its purpose.

The students were happy with themselves and one another again.

That group of students moved on. Several years later, after I returned from a vacation, my parents met me at the airport. As we were driving home, Mother asked me the usual questions about the trip—the weather, my experiences in general. There was a slight lull in the conversation. Mother gave Dad a sideways glance and simply said, "Dad?"

My father cleared his throat as he usually did before something important. "The Eklunds called last night," he began.

"Really?" I said. "I haven't heard from them in years. I wonder how Mark is."

Dad responded quietly. "Mark was killed in the war," he said. "The funeral is tomorrow, and his parents would like it if you could attend." To this day I can still point to the exact spot on I-494 where Dad told me about Mark.

I had never seen a serviceman in a military coffin before. Mark looked so handsome, so mature. All I could think at that moment was, Mark, I would give all the masking tape in the world if only you would talk to me.

The church was packed with Mark's friends. Chuck's sister sang "The Battle Hymn of the Republic." Why did it have to rain on the day of the funeral? It was difficult enough at the graveside. The pastor said the usual prayers, and the bugler played taps. One by one those who loved Mark took a last walk by the coffin and sprinkled it with holy water.

I was the last one to bless the coffin. As I stood there, one of the soldiers who had acted as pallbearer came up to me. "Were you Mark's math teacher?" he asked. I nodded as I continued to stare at the coffin. "Mark talked about you a lot," he said.

After the funeral, most of Mark's former classmates headed to Chuck's farmhouse for lunch. Mark's mother and father were there, obviously waiting for me. "We want to show you something," his father said, taking a wallet out of his pocket. "They found this on Mark when he was killed. We thought you might recognize it."

Opening the billfold, he carefully removed two worn pieces of notebook paper that had obviously been taped, folded and refolded many times. I knew without looking that the papers were the ones on which I had listed all the good things each of Mark's classmates had said about him. "Thank you so much for doing that," Mark's mother said. "As you can see, Mark treasured it."

Mark's classmates started to gather around us. Charlie smiled rather sheepishly and said, "I still have my list. It's in the top drawer of my desk at home." Chuck's wife said, "Chuck asked me to put his list in our wedding album." "I have mine too," Marilyn said. "It's in my diary." Then Vicki, another classmate, reached into her pocketbook, took out her wallet, and showed her worn and frazzled list to the group. "I carry this with me at all times," Vicki said without batting an eyelash. "I think we all saved our lists."

That's when I finally sat down and cried. I cried for Mark and for all his friends who would never see him again.

■ ■ ■

Wonder in the Air

Preview

Most parents really want to do a good job. They love their kids and try to do the right thing. The problem is, the right thing is not always obvious. As Jeff Gammage discovers, sometimes parents have to make up the rules as they go along.

Wonder in the Air

Jeff Gammage

When my wife and I had our first child, we established one firm parental rule:

No lies.

Our daughter, Jin Yu, spent her first two years in an orphanage in China, and we knew that as she grew, she would ask innumerable questions about her life there. We wanted to be able to answer from an established position of truth-telling.

For me, the "All the truth, all the time" policy extended onto the symbols and myths of the holidays.

Every April, I gladly helped fill a basket with candy rabbits and colored eggs for our daughter, and then for her new sister, but skipped the story of the Easter bunny. I avoided any mention of leprechauns, tried to ignore the tooth fairy.

Most of all, I was adamant about not telling Jin Yu tales about a certain red-suited fat man who spends every December 24 breaking into people's homes.

Of course, like the Grinch, I couldn't stop Christmas—or Santa Claus—from coming. Jin Yu absorbed a belief in Santa as if by osmosis. By age 4 she knew who he (allegedly) was, how he (purportedly) looked, and what he (supposedly) did.

I didn't want to ruin her fun, but also didn't want her to feel deceived later on.

So, I responded to her questions about the big man with what I liked to think of as precise and technically accurate versions of the literal truth—and what she would no doubt characterize as weasel words.

At the mall, we'd walk past a jolly Santa sitting upon a velvet throne.

"Is that really Santa?" my daughter would ask.

I'd reply with a lawyerly, "The people in line must think so."

The worst was when she wondered if Santa truly kept lists of children who behaved and misbehaved.

"That's the prevalent belief," I said.

By last Christmas Eve, I had done such an expert job of parenting, made such a successful effort to be truthful, that as I tucked my daughter into bed, she was confused and near tears.

"Daddy, will Santa"—here her voice almost broke—"bring me any presents?"

This was it, the question squarely placed, a moment that offered a stark choice between fable and fact, that demanded a reasoned response from a father grounded in principle. I looked at my adored child, her dark brown eyes threatening to overflow, knowing there was but one choice, and I made it:

I lied.

On Christmas Eve, the holy of holy nights, I lied to my 5-year-old daughter so fully, so deliberately and in such compelling detail that I nearly believed it myself.

"Darling, *of course* Santa is going to bring you presents. He would never overlook you. You're such a good girl [that part was true] that I know Santa will stop here. Listen, do you hear that sound outside? I think it's jingle bells! It must be his sleigh!"

Jin Yu turned to the window, hoping to glimpse a team of reindeer in flight, then lay back and drifted off, content, or at least relieved.

The next morning, she awoke to find that, sure enough, Santa had visited her home, proving his existence by magically delivering a wardrobe of princess gowns and dress-up shoes in exactly her size.

I think he left something for me as well: The power of a child's belief. A reminder that the best things in life cannot be seen with the naked eye. And that while there will be plenty of time for my daughter to ponder cold and painful truths, her time of wonder should be savored.

This year, fully 6, Jin Yu is happily preparing for Santa by drawing crayon snowscapes and discussing his impending arrival with friends. She counsels her 3-year-old sister, Zhao Gu, on the subtleties of naughty and nice.

Last week Jin Yu came to me with a very specific Christmas question, the sort that once again required a father's sure guidance: What kind of cookies should she leave for Santa on Christmas Eve?

I was firm in my response: Chocolate chip. Definitely, I told her, Santa likes chocolate chip.

■ ■ ■

The Yellow Ribbon

Preview

On the long bus ride from New York City to Florida, a story unfolds. It concerns a tired old ex-convict, the wife he'd left behind, and a famous old oak tree. For the young people who witnessed it, it was a love story they would never forget.

The Yellow Ribbon

Pete Hamill

They were going to Fort Lauderdale, the girl remembered later. There were six of them, three boys and three girls, and they picked up the bus at the old terminal on 34th Street, carrying sandwiches and wine in paper bags, dreaming of golden beaches and the tides of the sea as the gray cold spring of New York vanished behind them. Vingo was on board from the beginning.

As the bus passed through Jersey and into Philly, they began to notice that Vingo never moved. He sat in front of the young people, his dusty face masking his age, dressed in a plain brown ill-fitting suit. His fingers were stained

29

from cigarettes, and he chewed the inside of his lip a lot, frozen into some personal cocoon of silence.

Somewhere outside of Washington, deep into the night, the bus pulled into a Howard Johnson's, and everybody got off except Vingo. He sat rooted in his seat, and the young people began to wonder about him, trying to imagine his life: Perhaps he was a sea captain, maybe he had run away from his wife, he could be an old soldier going home. When they went back to the bus, the girl sat beside him and introduced herself.

"We're going to Florida," the girl said brightly. "You going that far?"

"I don't know." Vingo said.

"I've never been there," she said. "I hear it's beautiful."

"It is," he said quietly, as if remembering something he had tried to forget.

"You live there?"

"I did some time there in the Navy. Jacksonville."

"Want some wine?" she said. He smiled and took the bottle of Chianti and took a swig. He thanked her and retreated again into his silence. After a while, she went back to the others, as Vingo nodded in sleep.

In the morning they awoke outside another Howard Johnson's, and this time Vingo went in. The girl insisted that he join them. He seemed very shy and ordered black coffee and smoked nervously, as the young people chattered about sleeping on the beaches. When they went back on the bus, the girl sat with Vingo again, and after a while, slowly and painfully and with great hesitation, he began to tell his story. He had been in jail in New York for the last four years, and now he was going home.

"Four years!" the girl said. "What did you do?"

"It doesn't matter," he said with quiet bluntness. "I did it and I went to jail. If you can't do the time, don't do the crime. That's what they say, and they're right."

"Are you married?"

"I don't know."

"You don't know?" she said.

"Well, when I was in the can I wrote to my wife," he said. "I told her, I said, Martha, I understand if you can't stay married to me. I told her that. I said I was gonna be away a long time, and that if she couldn't stand it, if the kids kept askin' questions, if it hurt her too much, well, she could just forget me. Get a new guy—she's a wonderful woman, really something—and forget about me. I told her she didn't have to write me or nothing. And she didn't. Not for three and a half years."

"And you're going home now, not knowing?"

"Yeah," he said shyly. "Well, last week, when I was sure the parole was coming through I wrote her. I told her that if she had a new guy, I understood. But if she didn't, if she would take me back, she should let me know. We used to live in this town, Brunswick, just before Jacksonville, and there's a great big oak tree just as you come into town, a very famous tree, huge. I told her if she would take me back, she should put a yellow handkerchief on the tree, and I would get off and come home. If she didn't want me, forget it, no handkerchief, and I'd keep going on through."

"Wow," the girl said. "Wow."

She told the others, and soon all of them were in it, caught up in the approach of Brunswick, looking at the pictures Vingo showed them of his wife and three children, the woman handsome in a plain way, the children still unformed in a cracked, much-handled snapshot. Now they were twenty miles from Brunswick and the young people took over window seats on the right side, waiting for the approach of the great oak tree. Vingo stopped looking, tightening his face into the ex-con's mask, as if fortifying himself against still another disappointment. Then it was ten miles, and then five, and the bus acquired a dark hushed mood, full of silence, of absence, of lost years, of the woman's plain face, of the sudden letter on the breakfast table, of the wonder of children, of the iron bars of solitude.

Then suddenly all of the young people were up out of their seats, screaming and shouting and crying, doing small dances, shaking clenched fists in triumph and exaltation. All except Vingo.

Vingo sat there stunned, looking at the oak tree. It was covered with yellow handkerchiefs, twenty of them, thirty of them, maybe hundreds, a tree that stood like a banner of welcome blowing and billowing in the wind, turned into a gorgeous yellow blur by the passing bus. As the young people shouted, the old con slowly rose from his seat, holding himself tightly, and made his way to the front of the bus to go home.

■ ■ ■

From Shoebox
to Stardom

Preview

Emmanuel began
life in a war zone.
Physically disabled,
the baby boy was
abandoned by his
family. Years later, in a
new country he called
home, loved by a new
family, he challenged
listeners around the
world to "Imagine all
the people, living life
in peace."

From Shoebox to Stardom

Carol Siskin

It turned out to be two minutes and nine seconds that few who saw it will likely ever forget. But it all started out very simply.

"Welcome, Emmanuel. How old are you?" was the straightforward question from one of the judges on *The X-Factor*, the Australian television show that, like *American Idol*, seeks to discover the next great singing talent. "Well, I'm not exactly sure" came the surprising answer. And so began one of the most extraordinary moments in the history of the Australian program.

On this particular evening, contestants were competing in the "Judges' Auditions," the second stage of the five-step competition. In order to move on to the next stage and have any hope of being the eventual winner, a contestant would need to get a "thumbs-up" vote from three of the four judges. Many of these competitors would have compelling personal stories, proving that unusual talent is often found in unlikely places.

But Emmanuel's story was even more unlikely than most. For this young man was, as he put it, "from Australia via Iraq." He told the judges that he had been born in a war zone in Iraq and was abandoned by his family along with his older brother. There was a collective "Oh, no . . ." from the audience when he went on to say, "We were found in a shoebox by some nuns who took us to an orphanage. We had no birth certificates, no passports, nothing."

And, then, he explained, "An angel arrived at the orphanage" and took him and his brother back to Australia for surgery. Emmanuel was so strikingly handsome and so charismatic that until he said that, his physical disabilities didn't even seem particularly obvious. Yes, he had walked onto the stage very awkwardly, almost dragging his legs behind him. But, once on the stage, his personality was so electric and his looks so stunning that one almost forgot about his gait, his stunted arms, and his missing fingers. His face and smile made the young man irresistible.

And clearly, that had long been the case. While Moira Kelly had originally brought Emmanuel and his brother to Australia for surgery to address their multiple physical issues, she quickly became "mummy." Despite the challenge of taking on two handicapped boys, she adopted them both. As Emmanuel said with a laugh, "she kind of fell in love with us."

If this life story was almost beyond belief, so too was what came next. For now it was Emmanuel's time to perform. "I'm going to sing 'Imagine' by John Lennon," he announced. One of the judges could be heard saying, "Oh wow," perhaps anticipating that this was going to be something very special. And the slight gasp from the audience seemed to indicate that they knew it too.

When Emmanuel sang the first line of the song in a strong yet tender voice, it was instantly clear that he was a remarkable singer. The thousand or so audience members reacted by jumping to their feet. They began swaying to the music, also raising their hands above their heads as if in triumph. They seemed honored to be sharing this moment with an extraordinary young man who had overcome so many daunting obstacles to get to this place. The supposedly neutral judges were visibly moved, not just by

Emmanuel's obvious talent but also by his mere presence on the stage. One visibly fought back tears, and one held his head in his hands and whispered "Oh, my God." And when this young man who had been a child victim of a cruel war sang the words, "Imagine all the people living life in peace," the crowd could barely contain itself. The cheering became almost deafening, and cameras panning the audience revealed many eyes shining with tears.

The words of the song may have reminded people of the way the world should be. For a few magical minutes, Emmanuel and his song made everyone wish for a world in which we would all love each other the way the Australian woman came to love the two abandoned Iraqi boys. And people cheered and cried because they had been privileged to witness the power of love—a love that is greater than misfortune or war, a love that can help us rise above the countless problems of life.

The emotional response of the audience and the judges could only be topped by the reactions of Emmanuel's family, watching and cheering in the wings. His "angel" mother, Moira, and his brother, cousin and "auntie," all bursting with pride, cried tears of joy and kept repeating, "Listen to the audience, listen to the audience!" When, his "mum" embraced her other adoptive son, with his stunted arms wrapped as far as they could go around her neck, viewers witnessed both the power of love and the real meaning of "family."

With the roar of the crowd's standing ovation continuing, Emmanuel sang the concluding lines of the song:

> *"You may say that I'm a dreamer*
> *But I'm not the only one.*
> *I hope someday you'll join us*
> *And the world will be as one."*

The judges now jumped to their feet, erasing any doubt there might have been about Emmanuel's making it to the next round. Emmanuel's family embraced and cried with joy once more. "That's our boy," said his beaming "mum."

In his pre-performance interview, Emmanuel had talked about his dream of being a performer and what it would mean to him to win the competition. But to those watching in the audience and around the world—including the seven million people who eventually watched the segment on YouTube—Emmanuel was already a winner. And he and his devoted family provided an invaluable lesson to us all: that when we are surrounded and inspired by love, our dreams are all within reach.

■ ■ ■

To Tony Lopez, with Love

Preview

In this moving tribute to his late father, Steve Lopez remembers his dad's penny-pinching ways, his generosity, his humor, and his loyalty. The writer does more, though. He calls on society to re-think the way we deal with difficult, end-of-life issues.

To Tony Lopez, with Love

Steve Lopez

LA Times, February 22, 2012

My dad never called a tow truck. That would have cost too much.

It didn't matter where he broke down in his second-hand jalopies. Tony Lopez was a Depression-era guy who watched his wallet and dropped daily pocket change into a cigar box to pay for annual family vacations in Santa Cruz or Tahoe. When his car conked out, my dad called my Uncle Mike, who was cut from the same cloth. Mike would drive for miles and use a chain to tow my dad to safety, and they'd check junkyards for used parts and make the needed repairs themselves.

Remember the days of towing by chain, with sparks flying when the drooping links hit the pavement? That was my dad. It's a miracle he didn't go up in a ball of flames.

Tony Lopez didn't hire plumbers or landscapers. He did it himself or called friends, and he returned the favor when they needed help. He was frugal, for sure, but there wasn't much cushion in a bread truck driver's paycheck. Before checking into a motel, he was known to find out whether the bed could be taken apart so some of his brood could sleep on the box spring to save the cost of a bigger room. On a trip to Europe, my father, brother and I stayed in flop-houses and hovels near railroad stations, once sleeping in the bedroom of a house where the owner had just plucked a chicken and left feathers everywhere.

"That's where they get you!" he'd declare if soup and salad were not included in the price of a meal.

And yet for a guy who would drive 50 miles for a nickel discount on a gallon of gas, especially if they gave you juice glasses with every fill-up, my dad was always ticked off if I reached for the check at a restaurant. When I bought my first house, he insisted on helping with the down payment to lower my monthly burden. With his three kids and four grandchildren, he was as generous with his love as his money, sticking with us even when we screwed up.

Tony Lopez died the other day at the age of 83 after a long illness that he fought like a mule, literally hanging onto the rails of his bed to keep from being dragged into history. He used to bump into the undertaker around town, hold up his hand and say, "Not yet," as if he were waiting for a sale on funerals. But his time was finally up, and he went quietly Sunday morning, dying in his own home with my mother and sister at his side.

I want to thank him for the love and support, the memories, the sensibilities, the laughs.

Tony Lopez, a scrappy little four-sport high school athlete known as a fierce competitor, raised a daughter who inherited his fight. If you went by statistics, my sister Debbie would have been gone a couple of years ago, done in by ovarian cancer that spread to her brain. But she's still battling.

Tony Lopez, never too shy to clown around in a crazy wig or wacky hat, raised a son who became a comedian, inheriting my dad's ability to connect with everyone, including strangers. My dad got tears in his eyes laughing about the time my brother Johnny edited my Aunt Milly's bumper sticker from "Say No To Drugs, Yes to Burritos—New Mecca Cafe," so that it said "Say Yes to Drugs." Milly drove around like that for months, wondering why she got so many peculiar looks.

Tony Lopez didn't go to college and never moved out of the little town he grew up in, but he sent his first son to college on that once-abundant and adequately funded California dream of giving your kids greater opportunities than you'd ever had. The son went to San Jose State to become a journalist who shares his dad's suspicion of authority, and the journalist would like to thank his dad for this last gift—a story that has lent support to others, and perhaps some insights, on the hard choices around death and dying.

Those who have followed the tale of my dad's months-long decline, or have been through this themselves, know the anguish of decisions about life-extending medical procedures and where final days should be spent. I'd see but a shadow of my dad, curled up in half surrender, and want for him to slip away. Then he'd surprise me with a glance or a whispered "hello," and I didn't want to let go.

I came to appreciate the merits of palliative and hospice care, which help both patient and family prepare for the inevitable. But death is in charge and comes when it's ready, and after the hearse pulls away, an instant of relief gives way to a chill that creeps into your bones.

I believe more strongly than ever that everyone ought to have the option of doctor-assisted aid in dying. I can't tell you how many people have asked me why we keep loved ones alive with cruel limitations, but humanely end the suffering of animals.

Let Tony Lopez's passing stand as a call for doctors to be more up front in laying out the hard realities of medical limitations. And let it stand as a call for families to share their own attitudes with each other as to how much compromise is acceptable. Too many people are hanging on against their own wishes, only because they didn't make their feelings known in advance healthcare directives and other forms (which anyone can get from the Coalition for Compassionate Care of California, **coalitionccc.org**).

In his final days, my father was treated with grace and dignity by nurses and aides who grew up in Nigeria and Tonga, among other places, and they served our family and a noble profession well. And if my mother and sister were nuns, they would surely pass beatification and go directly to sainthood for the way they loved and cared for my father.

My heartfelt thanks, as well, to readers who have checked in by the hundreds with their own stories and words of support.

Peace, dad.

You had a heck of a good run.

The Love of a Dog

Preview

Dogs and humans—
they go together like
peanut butter and jelly.
How have two species,
so different from one
another, become such
close companions? In
this essay, the author
explores the beginning
of the dog-human bond
and presents examples
of how that bond has
only deepened over
time.

The Love of a Dog

Beth Johnson

There are so many kinds of love. There is the protective love of a mother for her baby; the fiery love of a couple in the first days of romance; the tender love of an adult caring for an aging parent. But of all the varieties of love in this world, maybe none are as pure and uncomplicated as the love of a dog for its special human.

Dogs and people have had a special bond for thousands of years. Some time after ancient man first noticed curious wolf puppies exploring near the campsite, he offered those puppies a bone. The puppies came nearer. Soon they were playing with the children and amusing the adults with their antics. As the puppies matured, they became useful as well. They guarded the campsite from intruders. They accompanied their people on hunting trips and helped to bring down and retrieve game. Man domesticated other animals to use for labor or food or clothing. But the dog's bond with humans remained unique. Somewhere along the long chain of history, the dog chose us. It turned its back on its wild wolf ancestry and became man's companion, protector, and friend.

It's easy to explain the affection of a coddled pet dog for its owner. When a dog has a warm place to sleep, good food to eat, and plenty of affection, it's tempting to think it is just taking advantage of its good fortune. But what about the half-starved dogs, cold and footsore, that cuddle with their homeless owners on city sidewalks? What about beaten dogs who, despite their sharp teeth and fighting ability, still lick the hand of their abuser? What about dogs that die in the defense of their owner's home or family? What about the dogs that gladly spend their lives working as guides for the blind, service dogs for the disabled, or K-9 officers for the police? That kind of behavior can only be described as unselfish love.

Stories of dogs that watch over lost children are common. Take the the story of 22-month old Tyler Jacobson, of South Carolina. On an April evening at around 8 p.m., Tyler slipped out of his house, wearing only a diaper. His mother called the police, who used a helicopter with an infrared sensing device to search for the missing toddler until after midnight, with no success. The search started up again at 7:30 a.m.. Shortly after that, searchers heard a dog barking frantically. They followed the sound and found Tyler, cold but unhurt, crying in the woods. The family's yellow Labrador mix was cuddled against him, keeping him warm, and barking for help.

Or think about 3-year-old Victoria Bensch, the little girl who wandered away from her Arizona home on a night when temperatures dipped below freezing. After fifteen hours, a helicopter pilot spotted her lying in a dry creek bed. Lying pressed against her was her dog Blue, an Australian Heeler. As rescuers approached the little girl, the dog growled protectively. "But once the dog realized we were there to help them out, he was very excited," the pilot said. "When it was time to go, he jumped right into the helicopter and was ready to go."

Other dogs have become famous for a love and loyalty that continued even after their owners' deaths. One of the most famous is the little Skye terrier known as Greyfriars Bobby.

Bobby's owner was a policeman in Edinburgh, Scotland. His name was John Gray, but he was generally known as "Old Jock." Old Jock had a tough beat (his assigned territory) to patrol. It included the Cattle Market and other areas where drunkenness and robbery were common. Old Jock needed a dog to help him, and he adopted Bobby when he was only six months old.

Soon Bobby and Old Jock were inseparable. When their work was done, they would often walk past Greyfriars Kirkyard (Churchyard) to a coffee house owned by Old Jock's friend William Ramsey. Man and dog always took the same seat, and Mrs. Ramsey would give Bobby a good meal.

Two years after adopting Bobby, Old Jock developed a terrible cough after patrolling in particularly cold, wet weather. He was diagnosed with tuberculosis. He was soon too weak to leave his bed. Bobby was lying at his feet when Old Jock died on February 8, 1857.

At Old Jock's funeral, Bobby sat with the family, and accompanied them to Greyfriars Kirkyard, where Old Jock was buried. The following morning, the church gardener found the little dog sleeping on his master's grave. Dogs were not allowed in the churchyard, so the gardener chased him away. But the next day Bobby was back, and the day after that. Eventually the gardener gave in and allowed him to stay.

Bobby spent the rest of his long life living in Greyfriars Kirkyard, keeping watch over Old Jock's grave. At 1 p.m. on the dot, he would run to Ramsey's coffee house, where the Ramseys would give him his daily meal. Then he would return to his watchplace.

Bobby became a local legend, and many people attempted to take him into their homes to adopt him. Even Queen Victoria paid him a visit. He was polite to all of them, but he was not interested in a new home. The faithful little dog would not leave his master's grave. He would watch over Old Jock for the rest of his days.

In January 1872, Bobby died. The current owner of the coffee house and other friends gathered his body and buried it in a flower bed just outside the churchyard. A monument erected in his honor reads, "Greyfriars Bobby. Died 14th January 1872, aged 16 years. Let his loyalty and devotion be a lesson to us all."

Let his loyalty and devotion be a lesson to us all. As anyone who has been loved by a dog can attest, these words are a fitting tribute to the best friends human beings have ever had.

■ ■ ■

The Most Hateful Words

Preview

"Forgive and forget"
are words easier
to say than to put
into practice. For
Amy Tan and her
mother, wounded by
a lifetime of conflict,
the words took on
concrete meaning in an
unexpectedly healing
way.

The Most Hateful Words
Amy Tan

The most hateful words I have ever said to another human being were to my mother. I was sixteen at the time. They rose from the storm in my chest, and I let them fall in a fury of hailstones: "I hate you. I wish I were dead. . . ."

I waited for her to collapse, stricken by what I had just said. She was still standing upright, her chin tilted, her lips stretched in a crazy smile. "Okay, maybe I die too," she said between huffs. "Then I no longer be your mother!" We had many similar exchanges. Sometimes she actually tried to kill herself by running into the street, holding a knife to her throat. She too had storms in her chest. And what she aimed at me was as fast and deadly as a lightning bolt.

For days after our arguments, she would not speak to me. She tormented me, acted as if she had no feelings for me whatsoever. I was lost to her. And because of that, I lost, battle after battle, all of them: the times she criticized me, humiliated me in front of others, forbade me to do this or that without even listening to one good reason why it should be the other way. I swore to myself I would never forget these injustices. I would store them, harden my heart, make myself as impenetrable as she was.

I remember this now, because I am also remembering another time, just a few years ago. I was forty-seven, had become a different person by then, had become a fiction writer, someone who uses memory and imagination. In fact, I was writing a story about a girl and her mother, when the phone rang.

It was my mother, and this surprised me. Had someone helped her make the call? For a few years now, she had been losing her mind through Alzheimer's disease. Early on, she forgot to lock her door. Then she forgot where she lived. She forgot who many people were and what they had meant to her. Lately, she could no longer remember many of her worries and sorrows.

"Amy-ah," she said, and she began to speak quickly in Chinese. "Something is wrong with my mind. I think I'm going crazy."

I caught my breath. Usually she could barely speak more than two words at a time. "Don't worry," I started to say.

"It's true," she went on. "I feel like I can't remember many things. I can't remember what I did yesterday. I can't remember what happened a long time ago, what I did to you. . . ." She spoke as a drowning person might if she had bobbed to the surface with the force of will to live, only to see how far she had already drifted, how impossibly far she was from the shore.

She spoke frantically: "I know I did something to hurt you."

"You didn't," I said. "Don't worry."

"I did terrible things. But now I can't remember what. . . . And I just want to tell you . . . I hope you can forget, just as I've forgotten."

I tried to laugh so she would not notice the cracks in my voice. "Really, don't worry."

"Okay, I just wanted you to know."

After we hung up, I cried, both happy and sad. I was again that sixteen-year-old, but the storm in my chest was gone.

My mother died six months later. By then she had bequeathed to me her most healing words, as open and eternal as a clear blue sky. Together we knew in our hearts what we should remember, what we can forget.

■ ■ ■

Jack and Mark

Preview

Friendships are sometimes formed in the most unlikely places—like a hospital cafeteria. That's where Jack and Mark met, two men who, externally, had little in common. But when Mark saw Jack's pain, and Jack felt Mark's caring, something special happened.

Jack and Mark

Michael Vitez

Mark Harris works the grill in the cafeteria at Abington Memorial Hospital.

Jack Lawlor's wife was dying. He was at the hospital day after day, hoping she'd get better, and every day he'd go into the cafeteria for a steak sandwich.

Mark knows all the regulars, the doctors and nurses. He noticed Jack after a few days in line and concluded that he was visiting a sick relative. Mark tried to be cheerful to him in line, and do what he could—give him extra steak on his sandwich.

Jack was not too lost in grief to notice how hard Mark was working at the grill, hustling, juggling many orders at once, always being cheerful to him—and very generous with the steak.

Mark is a black man, raised in Philadelphia in a series of foster homes, now 42. Jack is a white man, 80, from Hatboro, many years ago the retail advertising manager for this very newspaper.

One day, after lunch, Jack was waiting outside the cafeteria for the elevator back to intensive care. Mark walked by, stopped, asked Jack why he was at Abington.

Jack told him his wife had suffered a second stroke and was declining.

"I could feel his pain," said Mark, "because my own foster mother had just died. She raised me till I was 10. She was the easiest woman in the world to please."

Though the city had moved Mark to a different foster family and expected them to sever contact, he stayed close to her until her last breath.

"He was telling me about her, and tears are coming down," said Jack. "I tell him about my wife, and I'm crying."

Mark rode up the elevator with Jack, sat with him for a while in the ICU.

Next thing, Mark was going up every day, taking balloons, candy, a kind word. "Mark used to bring me a little dish of ice cream, whatever I needed," said Jack. "He's crying along with us all the time. Just a welcome stranger in our lives.

"I was down getting coffee," Jack said. "I

told him it looked like it was going to be soon, and sure enough, he was up there, along with a religious person, in the room, and a doctor. They said she would be passing in another minute. There's Mark with us, holding hands, in his white outfit from the grill. He's up there with us until she passed away.

"The hospice people, they were very nice," said Jack. "They said you'd get follow-up calls, and I did get one or two follow-up calls from hospice, asking how I was doing. The person who called me every day was Mark. He started calling me Pops. 'Are you OK, Pops?' 'Yeah, I'm OK.' 'Are you sure?' The person who called me regularly for at least a week or more was Mark."

Jack would come back to Abington, to the cafeteria, every few weeks, right around Mark's break time, and have a cup of coffee with him, meet his hospital friends, learn all about his life, give him advice.

About two years after his wife died, Jack was in the hospital himself. It was sudden. He couldn't alert Mark.

"Next morning came," said Jack, "and I heard Mark out in the hallway. He has a lot of spies, and somebody told him I was there. I'm getting a transfusion. He's saying something to the nurse at the desk."

"Who are you looking for?" she asks Mark.

"I'm looking for my Pops."

"No, I don't think he's here," the nurse

replies. There were no older black men on that floor.

"Well, let me go look."

"You can't go looking into patients' rooms."

Mark finds Jack.

"Hey, Pops! How about a steak sandwich?"

A year later, Jack was visiting Mark in the Abington cafeteria and saw Dick Jones, who was then the hospital CEO. Mark was still behind the grill, not yet on break.

Jack introduced himself to the CEO. "What brings you here?" the CEO asked.

"I have a friend here," Jack replied. "He's the greatest spokesman for your organization."

A year ago, when Mark's sister died, Jack went to the funeral. It was at a big Baptist church in West Philly, near 57th and Arch. Jack estimates there were 500 people there, and he was the only white person. Mark was following the casket in a procession up to the altar. He stopped, walked over to Jack, gave him a hug.

Their friendship has been going strong for six years. Mark writes poetry, shares it with Jack, who says, "It's unreal. It's beautiful."

Jack mainly listens to Mark, gives him advice, tries to persuade him to quit smoking.

"We're like father and son," says Mark.

Jack already had a son named Mark.

Now he has two.

■ ■ ■

We Found Our Son
on the Subway

Preview

Danny and Peter had
been a couple for three
years when a stunning
discovery kicked off
a chain of events
neither man had ever
anticipated. Along the
way, the pair learned
much about love, about
themselves, and about
the power of following
a hunch.

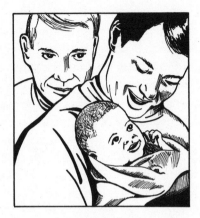

We Found Our Son on the Subway

Peter Mercurio

The story of how Danny and I were married last July in a Manhattan courtroom, with our son, Kevin, beside us, began 12 years earlier, in a dark, damp subway station.

Danny called me that day, frantic. "I found a baby!" he shouted. "I called 911, but I don't think they believed me. No one's coming. I don't want to leave the baby alone. Get down here and flag down a police car or something." By nature Danny is a remarkably calm person, so when I felt his heart pounding through the phone line, I knew I had to run.

When I got to the A/C/E subway exit on Eighth Avenue, Danny was still there, waiting for help to arrive. The baby, who had been left on the ground in a corner behind the turnstiles, was light-brown-skinned and quiet, probably about a day old, wrapped in an oversize black sweatshirt.

In the following weeks, after family court had taken custody of "Baby ACE," as he was nicknamed, Danny told the story over and over again, first to every local TV news station, then to family members, friends, co-workers and acquaintances. The story spread like an urban myth: You're never going to believe what my friend's cousin's co-worker found in the subway. What neither of us knew, or could have predicted, was that Danny had not just saved an abandoned infant; he had found our son.

Three months later, Danny appeared in family court to give an account of finding the baby. Suddenly, the judge asked, "Would you be interested in adopting this baby?" The question stunned everyone in the courtroom, everyone except for Danny, who answered, simply, "Yes."

"But I know it's not that easy," he said.

"Well, it can be," assured the judge before barking off orders to commence with making him and, by extension, me, parents-to-be.

My first reaction, when I heard, went something like: "Are you insane? How could you say yes without consulting me?" Let's just say I nailed the "jerk" part of knee-jerk.

In three years as a couple, we had never discussed adopting a child. Why would we? Our lives were not geared for child-rearing. I was an aspiring playwright working as a part-time word processor, and Danny was a respected yet wildly underpaid social worker. We had a roommate sleeping behind a partition in our living room to help pay the rent. Even if our financial and logistical circumstances had been different, we knew how many challenges gay couples usually faced when they want to adopt. And while Danny had patience and selflessness galore, I didn't. I didn't know how to change a diaper, let alone nurture a child.

But here was fate, practically giving us a baby. How could we refuse? Eventually, my fearful mind spent, my heart seized control to assure me I could handle parenthood.

A caseworker arranged for us to meet the baby at his foster home in early December. Danny held the fragile baby first, then placed him in my arms. In order to protect myself from future heartache, I had convinced myself I could not, and would not, become inextricably attached. I didn't trust the system and was sure there would be obstacles. But with the baby's eyes staring up at me, and all the innocence and hope he represented, I, like Danny, was completely hooked.

The caseworker told us that the process, which included an extensive home study and parenting classes, could take up to nine months.

We'd have ample time to rearrange our lives and home for a baby. But a week later, when Danny and I appeared in front of the judge to officially state our intention to adopt, she asked, "Would you like him for the holiday?"

What holiday? Memorial Day? Labor Day? She couldn't have meant Christmas, which was only a few days away.

And yet, once again, in unison this time, we said yes. The judge grinned and ordered the transition of the baby into our custody. Our nine-month window of thoughtful preparation was instantly compacted to a mere 36 hours. We were getting a baby for Christmas.

We spent that year as foster parents while our caseworker checked up on us and the baby's welfare. During that time we often wondered about the judge. Did she know Danny was a social worker and therefore thought he would make a good parent? Would she have asked him to adopt if she knew Danny was gay and in a relationship? At the final hearing, after she had signed the official adoption order, I raised my hand. "Your honor, we've been wondering why you asked Danny if he was interested in adopting?"

"I had a hunch," she just said. "Was I wrong?" And with that she rose from her chair, congratulated us, and exited the courtroom.

And that was how we left it, as Baby ACE became Kevin, and grew from an infant to a boy. That is, until 2011, when New York State allowed Danny and me to legally marry.

"Why don't you ask the judge who performed my adoption to marry you and dad?" Kevin suggested one morning on our walk to school.

"Great idea," I replied. "Would you like to meet her?"

"Sure. Think she'd remember me?"

"There's only one way to find out."

After dropping Kevin off, I composed a query letter and sent it to the catchall e-mail address listed for the Manhattan family court. Within hours, a court attorney called to say that, of course, the judge remembered us, and was thrilled by the idea of officiating at our marriage. All we had to do was pick a date and time.

When we ventured back to family court for the first time in over ten years, I imagined that the judge might be nervous to come face to face with the results of one of her placement decisions —what if Kevin wasn't happy and wished he had different parents? Kevin was nervous too. When he was a toddler, Danny and I made him a storybook that explained how we became a family, and it included an illustration of the judge, gavel in hand. A character from his book was about to jump off the page as a real person. What if she didn't approve of the way he had turned out?

Kevin reached out to shake her hand.

"Can I give you a hug?" she asked. When they separated, the judge asked Kevin about school, his interests, hobbies, friends, and expressed her delight that we were there.

When we finally remembered the purpose of the visit, and Danny and I moved into position to exchange vows, I reflected on the improbable circumstances that delivered all of us to this moment. We weren't supposed to be there, two men, with a son we had never dreamed of by our side, getting married by a woman who had changed and enriched our lives more than she would ever know. But there we were, thanks to a fateful discovery and a judicious hunch.

■ ■ ■

Graduating to Freedom

Preview

A young man graduates from medical school. It would be a proud moment for any family. But what Harley Rotbart's father, a survivor of the Nazi death camps, experienced that day went far beyond a parent's pride. Witnessing his reaction allowed Harley to fully understand his father.

Graduating to Freedom

Harley A. Rotbart

It was May 1979, and pouring rain, so my Cornell medical school graduation had to be moved indoors to one of the Lincoln Center auditoriums. My mom and dad and younger brother were there all the way from Denver to watch me receive my diploma and take the Hippocratic Oath as a new doctor. This was my parents' first time in New York. Dad hadn't traveled much since the "big trip" to America from Poland. He was an Auschwitz survivor (No. 142178 tattooed on his arm) who lost his parents and sister in the concentration camps. My father had enough strength left to be selected for labor by the Nazis, and survived until liberation.

Still, true liberation didn't come until that rainy graduation weekend in New York.

Dad was a fruit peddler in Denver: Max's Mobile Market. Awestruck is an understatement for his reaction to New York. The World Trade Center, Statue of Liberty, Broadway, and a fruit stand on nearly every corner. He was the most brilliant fruit peddler in the history of fruit peddling, the smartest man I ever knew. Deprived of a high school education when the Nazis raided his town of Klodowa, he came to America years later as an apprehensive, thickly accented refugee from the unspeakable horrors of Europe. Despite many years in America, the emotional scars were still there. He had a sense of inferiority and was intimidated by those around him who had an education. He was always socially self-conscious, acutely afraid of standing out for his lack of accomplishments. Within his circle of family and friends, Dad was proud of who he was and what he had overcome. We knew he was proud of us, too. My journalist-to-be brother and I had chosen professions Dad respected and admired. But outside my father's inner circle, he was introverted, stoic, reserved. He would withdraw in the company of those who didn't have to make their livelihoods on a fruit truck, and always regarded himself as the immigrant in the room.

On cue, the graduation speakers read their parts: "It was only four short years ago . . . ," "The experiences we had, the friendships we made." "Pomp and Circumstance" played, tassels were flipped, mortarboards flew in the air. The emotion I felt during the ceremony, however, was nothing compared with what happened afterward when I waded through the crowd to find my family near the center of the lobby. Hundreds of doctors, parents of doctors, friends of doctors and professors of doctors were milling about. This should have been the ultimate intimidating environment for my father. After hugs from my brother and Mom, I moved on to Dad. What happened at that moment I will never forget. Crying loudly, Dad fell to his knees in what can only be described as a total emotional breakdown. He shook and shivered and sobbed. People all around turned to stare, but he didn't notice or didn't care. The usual self-consciousness was gone. As I dropped to my knees to face him, he held me like never before. Everyone backed away to give us space; a few applauded. Strangers took pictures. Dad and I stayed on our knees, crying and hugging for a long time, until we both had the strength to stand up. Then, holding onto each other and to my mom and brother, we made our way out of the auditorium. We didn't stop at the reception for cookies or punch. We just kept walking until we felt the rain on our faces.

Only later did I fully realize what had happened. On that day, and again in a similar scene at my brother's journalism school ceremony the next year, Dad was liberated from Auschwitz. He was no longer "142178," a Nazi victim. My father could now stand face to face with doctors, journalists and other accomplished Americans. Although uneducated himself, he had educated his kids, and that was plenty good enough. Better than good enough: it was great. No longer bound by the restraints life had forced on him, he reveled in what this new country had given him. He reveled in his family and in his fruit truck. He reveled in personally defeating Hitler. At his sons' graduations, he graduated to freedom.

Three years after my graduation, Dad died from pancreatic cancer. He never knew his grandchildren but would have been very proud of them. He missed all of their graduations, but with each one we again celebrated Dad's liberation. But for his strength, courage and sacrifice, none of us would have been here to collect our diplomas.

■ ■ ■

The Christmas Gift

Preview

One moment the young family was on a happy holiday journey. The next, they were lost, worried, and afraid for the safety of their baby son. Lights in the distance guided this modern-day Mary and Joseph to a place of warmth and angelic generosity.

The Christmas Gift

Andrew Scrimgeour

We never expected that we would want to be anywhere but in Denver for Christmas. But that year, when our first child arrived in August, my wife and I knew we had to go to California and show him off to my parents, brothers, and sisters, all of whom had long despaired that we would ever start a family.

We hadn't been averse to having children. We love them and hoped to have several. Just not right away. Our postponement stretched to 13 years as graduate degrees and careers consumed our attention.

Like many who put off starting a family, we were in no hurry to surrender our freedom. But more than that, we were intimidated by parenthood. The idea of taking on the responsibility of a new life was daunting. Could we be worthy of such trust?

When we finally managed to put aside those fears and embrace the challenge, we were reminded that we were not fully in charge of our strategic plan. A miscarriage intervened, compounding our worries and extending the delay. So when Drew arrived, safe and sound, defying the worries of his mid-30s parents, the euphoria that set in had to be shared across state lines.

Rather than head directly west, we decided to take a scenic route south through the snow-pocked plateaus of New Mexico and Arizona to Southern California. North of Los Angeles we would visit the Danish village of Solvang, famous for its Christmas splendor, and then head up the coast to our destination in Sonoma County.

Packing for the trip required some ingenuity since the space-gulping paraphernalia of our 4-month-old had to fit into our toy-size car, a yellow Volkswagen bug. The car seat alone took up most of the back seat, so diaper bags, the collapsible stroller and Christmas gifts filled every niche. At the urging of friends, who knew of our lack of winter travel experience, we stashed a large candle, matches and water in the rear window compartment—a safety precaution should we become marooned in the desolate stretches of the Southwest.

Once under way we motored south on the Interstate, talking nonstop, reveling in every gurgle from the newest family member and delighting in the ribbons of snow skittering across the pavement.

By midafternoon I was ready for a change and asked Dot if she would take the wheel so I could read. Popping a Dramamine to avoid motion sickness, I dived into my book. Not surprisingly, my drug of choice soon closed the curtain on my literary intentions. Before I drifted off, I asked Dot to rouse me when we were near Albuquerque.

Several hours later I awoke with a start. Something was amiss. The sky was growing dark and the sun was all wrong, setting to my right when it should have been in my face.

"Didn't we turn west at Albuquerque?" I asked.

"No," Dot replied. "I woke you when I saw the signs, but you just grunted and went back to sleep. So I kept going."

I had no idea where we were—just somewhere in the desert south of Albuquerque. It was almost dark. Snow was swirling in the headlights, the temperature had plummeted, and I could feel the muscle of the wind against the car. Then I noticed the fuel gauge, and any hint of drowsiness evaporated. As though registering our final grade for a course in parental preparedness, the needle hovered on E—E for effort, E for empty.

Consulting the map confirmed it was unlikely that we were close to a town or gas station, and no one had passed us for some time. Nothing was in sight, only sagebrush and the distant mountains. The knowledge that we had emergency supplies offered little consolation. Where was the bidding star of Bethlehem when we needed it? We tried to keep panic at bay, but we knew we had put our baby at risk.

I shuddered to think that back in Denver on the morning of Drew's birth, I had been so fervent in my resolve to be a good father. I had made promises to him when he was barely dry, as I walked and rocked him for over an hour, while Dot wrestled out of the anesthesia. I nuzzled him, talked to him, sang to him and made promises—a good life, a full life, red wagons, sleds, books, zoos, milk with graham crackers smeared with butter.

Yet on the way to his first Christmas tree, I was already jeopardizing his life by failing at the most basic of parental duties: providing warmth and shelter.

We took the first road that seemed to lead northwest and after a while were rewarded by flickers of light in the distance. We turned in their direction at the first chance and soon arrived at a string of bare bulbs dangling over a barbed-wire enclosure.

Several trucks were parked inside the fence, each branded with white letters that read, "Bureau of Indian Affairs." We were, as it turned out, on the Laguna Indian Reservation. Beyond the security fence we could see a dozen small cement-block houses, a pickup in front of each. I pulled in beside the closest truck and stepped out into the snow. With that movement, I set off the village canine alarm system: dogs began to growl and bark, curtains parted, and shadows peered out. The VW intruders had been spotted.

Keeping an eye on the snarling sentinels, I knocked on the door of the nearest house.

It opened slightly to reveal a small boy. I explained our plight. Was gasoline available nearby?

Peeking through the crack, he pointed to the house opposite his.

Soon I was retelling our story to the man who answered that door. I had just said that my wife and baby were in the car when a woman shoved the man aside, opened the door fully and asked, "You have a baby in the car?"

I said that I did, and that his mother was in the car, too. "Get them in the house right now," she said. "They'll freeze to death out there!"

As soon as the three of us felt the warmth of the house and introductions were made, our host offered to drive me in his truck to the gas station at the reservation store several miles away. If we hurried, he urged, we could get there before it closed.

Out on the road he wasn't bashful with the gas pedal, and soon we were filling two five-gallon cans.

On the way back, several pickups passed us at high speed, one recklessly chasing another, horn blaring. My host solemnly explained that they were Laguna teenagers, that his son was probably among them and they were surely drinking, too.

"Our kids are trapped here," he said. "They won't leave the reservation and get a good education. They waste their money on cars, trucks, booze and girls. I worry about their future."

He talked for a while about such fears, like the toxic mine tailings he knew his son and his friends had been exposed to, and as he spoke I felt a kinship with him that would have eluded me only four months earlier. He was a father, I was a father; we had children to worry about. But whereas I was just starting on this path, full of joy and hope for my son, he was much further along, facing real threats and shouldering grave concerns.

When we arrived back at the house, I found Drew on a blanket on the living-room floor smiling contentedly at the children who were entertaining him in the light of a Christmas tree. Across the room, Dot was sitting at the table eating supper with our hostess. The woman rose and, pointing to a chair, said, "That's your place." She set plates of ham and scalloped potatoes in front of her husband and me, and the four of us dined and traded in a universal currency: stories about our children.

We stayed much too long at the table, but oases of kindness are difficult to leave. As we made our goodbyes, I was at a loss as to how to say thank you without blundering and insulting them. So as I shook our host's hand, I gave him a $10 bill, saying that while we could not begin to repay his family for their generosity, I at least wanted to reimburse him for his own gas.

He took the money and thanked me with the grace of a career diplomat. Then he stepped toward Dot, who was holding Drew, and carefully tucked the money under Drew's blanket. "I haven't had the chance to get your son a Christmas gift," he said. "Would you do it for me?"

And with that final kindness, we headed west into the darkness.

■ ■ ■

Love

Preview

If you're not involved in a romantic affair, does that mean there's no love in your life? That's crazy talk, says Lisa Scottoline. The world is bursting with different kinds of love. All you have to do is reach out and take it!

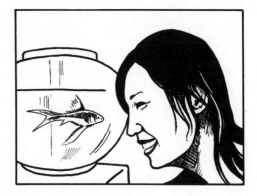

Love

Lisa Scottoline

Whenever Valentine's Day comes up, the newspaper, TV, and stores are full of heart-shaped candy boxes, roses, and jewelry for "that special someone." The holiday has become a celebration of romantic love, and that's great if you're in a romance or you're married, which is like having an automatic valentine.

But not everyone is so lucky.

There are plenty of people who aren't seeing someone right now, which is code for haven't had a date in 55 years. Like me. And that's okay, every day except Valentine's Day.

Single people feel like losers on Valentine's Day. They're left out of the hearts and candy. They become wallflowers at the party of life.

This is sad, and wrong. I think it's time to revisit the way we think about Valentine's Day. So welcome to another trademark Scottoline time-to-change-things story, wherein my bossy and controlling nature works to my advantage, for once.

To begin with, I did some research, and I learned that St. Valentine's Day was intended to celebrate a loving man, a priest so sweet, giving, and devout that he became a saint. Historically, his day had nothing to do with romance. In fact, it wasn't until the Middle Ages, when Geoffrey Chaucer wrote a poem entitled *The Parliament of Foules*, that St. Valentine's Day became associated with romantic love.

Aha! So the link between Valentine's Day and romance is pure fiction. Chaucer made it up, and trust me, he did it to move some poems. Sex sells. Romance novels are bestsellers for a reason, and even my books have sex scenes, which I write from memory.

And now I forget.

Given that the history of the holiday is so sketchy, I feel free to write on a clean slate. In other words, I can make it up, too. And if you ask me, Valentine's Day is really about love. Not only romantic love, but also just plain love. And if you're not married or seeing someone, you can still have love in your life.

Observe.

In my case, I have tons of love in my life. I love my kid, my family, and my friends. I love the people I work with. I love my readers. I love my dogs, cats, and pony. I love spaghetti. I love opera. I love books. I love Brad Pitt in *Legends of the Fall.*

In short, I love.

If I were going to improve on that maxim of Descartes, "I think, therefore I am," I'd say, "I love, therefore I am." Or instead of Pope's saying, "To err is human," I'd go with, "To love is human." Plus I agree completely with that great philosopher James Taylor, who tells us to "shower the people you love with love."

So I propose that, on Valentine's Day, we celebrate love. Shower the people you love with love. Don't take each other for granted. Recognize that we grow more valuable to each other as time passes, not less. Raise a glass to someone you love, in celebration of an emotion that powers our best intentions, leads to our greatest happiness, and gives us the stories of the world's greatest operas, movies, and novels.

In addition to *Gossip Girl.*

Now, there may be some of you reading this who have no one. Maybe you've lost someone, or they're far away, and you're left hiding in your house or apartment, waiting for Valentine's Day to pass.

Here's my advice to you:

Find the love in your life, because it's all around you. And if you can't find it, make it yourself.

Make love.

And by that, I don't mean **match.com**.

I mean adopt a dog and love it. Buy a pretty collar and walk it around the block. A cat works, too. Cats like pretty collars, even though they're too proud to say so. Or get a fish. There's no shame in love you can buy, even if it has scales. I don't think goldfish get enough credit. Not everybody can look good in orange.

Or read a book that everyone says is great. You'll find a story you love, and maybe an author. Or if you don't like to read, go see *Legends of the Fall*. You'll love Brad Pitt, whether you're a man or a woman.

And if none of that appeals to you, volunteer at a shelter or a hospital. Cook a meal for the parents at a Ronald McDonald House, like a friend of mine did.

Because the thing about love is that we can't control whether we get it, but we can control whether we give it.

And each feels as good as the other.

Your heart doesn't know whether it's loving a man, a TV show, or a guppy. If your heart were that smart, it would be your brain.

All your heart knows is that it's full and happy, and you will feel alive and human.

And next time, you will have a wonderful Valentine's Day.

And, better yet, a wonderful life.

■ ■ ■

Promises That Bend Without Breaking

Preview

Theirs was a marriage that was adventurous, full of travel and surprises. Then came a surprise that neither of them had dreamed of. Together, they began yet another journey, one that would call for a new kind of love.

Promises That Bend
Without Breaking

Robert St. Amant

In December my wife and I moved out of our
house into an independent-living apartment.
Walking through the building, you might take it
for a well-kept hotel, until you notice the handrails
lining the hallways, the nursing assistants in the
common areas, and the people pushing walkers
in front of them rather than pulling luggage carts
behind them. The average resident is close to 80
years old.

The end of the year brought a stream of
visitors. One afternoon we joined the other
residents to meet with fourth-graders who shyly

handed us candy canes and Christmas cards they had made. A quartet of a cellist and three violinists, their instruments marked with colored tape to help with the fingering, played for us on another day.

In the common dining room, with chairs and tables pushed out of the way, we have watched young ballet students dancing parts of "The Nutcracker." We have listened to a teenage harpist and sung Christmas carols accompanied by a visiting pianist.

I'm not sure I belong here. You'll occasionally hear others say the same thing, but it's different for me. I'm in good health, physically and mentally, and I work full time. I just turned 50.

My wife, a year younger, is the reason we're here.

We've been married 28 years, most of them carefree, some even exciting. In our first year together, we were living in Texas. I found out about a job opening at a satellite office of the company I worked for. I called my wife on the phone.

"What would you think of moving to Germany?" I asked.

"Sure," she said.

Six weeks later we walked into a small apartment in Moosburg, a small town just outside Munich. We spent the next five years in Germany, exploring Europe during weekends and holidays. We discovered we were within a day's drive of

Paris, Amsterdam, Berlin and Vienna, and we made those trips.

The evening before my birthday one year, my wife met me in the Munich train station on my return from a business trip. She pulled two suitcases from a locker and told me we were booked on a night train to Florence. Sometimes we'd take long driving trips through the countryside, my wife navigating with a map.

We had no destination in mind, but it was good to know where we were, if not where we were going. We'd eventually happen upon a small village with a guesthouse, perhaps on a picturesque town square, for food and drink and lodging. Our lives were open-ended.

Eventually we moved back to the United States. I went to graduate school in Massachusetts, earned a Ph.D. in computer science, and landed a job as a university professor in North Carolina. We bought a house with a swimming pool on the outskirts of Raleigh.

My wife found her calling in the craft of weaving: She'd occasionally sell a scarf or table runner on consignment, and once she saw her work appear in a national weaving magazine. The wanderlust struck us now and then. We spent my sabbatical year living in Southern California and talked about the possibility of moving back to Europe at some point. But we had settled down.

On a summer afternoon almost seven years ago, we were in the swimming pool. It was my wife's 43rd birthday. We were talking about where we'd go to dinner when she became quiet for a while. She slid off her float into the water, face down, and didn't come up for air. I pulled her out of the pool and called 911.

A few hours later, in the emergency room, a doctor told me my wife had had a seizure caused by brain tumors.

Late that night my wife had regained consciousness in her hospital room. She could speak, and she even smiled. A neurosurgeon talked with both of us, though he said that my wife was heavily medicated and wouldn't remember our conversation later.

The M.R.I.s showed three meningiomas, tumors in the membrane surrounding the brain. The doctor described them being the sizes of a walnut, a cherry, and a plum. They would need to be removed by surgery.

"What will you put in their place?" my wife asked.

"Nothing," he said. "The brain and its fluids will expand to fill the space."

"Will I be smarter then?"

The doctor and I laughed, while my wife just looked puzzled. It was a rare bright moment in the neurological intensive care unit.

The tumors were benign. After two surgeries and a painful recovery it seemed that life might return to normal. (Almost. One unexpected side effect was epilepsy, with seizures putting my wife in the hospital for up to a week at a time.)

She and I talked about the future, what we would do with our lives. We no longer had forever. My wife went back to work two or three days a week but devoted most of her free time to her crafts of weaving and embroidery.

I had never stopped working; in my spare time I wrote a popular science book, and my wife gave it a fitting title: *Computing for Ordinary Mortals.* We still traveled. We visited friends and family in other states, and we spent a summer month on the island of Madeira.

"This would be a good place for us," my wife said.

I agreed; I talked with a friend at the University of Madeira about job possibilities.

But on an annual checkup, my wife's M.R.I.s showed new brain tumors. This time the treatment was radiation, and she never fully recovered.

She became absent-minded, sometimes searching for ordinary words—glass, broom, table—for up to a minute in conversation. She lost track of time. She began to fall down.

"When are we going home?" she'd ask, and I'd walk around the room to point out the lamp she had brought back from Venice, the antique floor loom in the corner, and her fabrics hanging on the walls. We were already home.

By fall of last year, her dementia was comparable to mid-stage Alzheimer's disease, and it only rarely departed. Neurologists and neurosurgeons ran tests and suggested treatments, to no effect. On our last visit several months ago, her neurologist said that it would be surprising to see any improvement over time.

We talked, then, while my wife still had lucid periods. In the past we'd had fun with idle questions about the future.

"If we could live anywhere in the world, where would it be?" or "What would we do with a million dollars?"

This time it was more serious: "What will we do if you don't remember who I am?" We agreed that staying together was the most important thing. In sickness and in health, after all.

The solution seemed to be a place that caters to people with my wife's condition. The apartment is as familiar as I can make it. Our furniture is arranged to match our old house. Sometimes we sit in the living room and look through our photo albums. I bring out examples of my wife's weaving and embroidery for her to turn over in her hands. We socialize with the other residents whenever we have the chance.

One sunny day we were walking outside after lunch. In the parking lot we passed by a small blue convertible.

"That's a nice car," my wife said. Occasionally she speaks without prompting, but that's becoming rare.

"It is," I said. "What do you like about it?"

"It's a pretty color."

"Would you like to go for a ride?"

"Sure."

We walked to the passenger door and I opened it.

She looked confused. "Is this our car?"

"Yes." My wife had arranged for us to buy the car from one of her friends six months earlier. "It's O.K.," I said. "We haven't had it for long."

"I thought you were joking," she said.

"I thought you were joking. Do you want to go somewhere?"

"No."

Sometimes I think about the vows my wife and I made to each other, 28 years ago and then again last summer. We're different people than we once were. Does that make breaking a promise easier?

Last summer I said: "You can trust me. I'll always tell you the truth about what's happening."

Today I tell her small, comforting lies. Some promises, though, aren't just things you say or intend to do; they're about what kind of person you are. That makes it easier to decide what's right.

My wife and I were recently sitting with a group of older women, drinking coffee. One leaned over to me and whispered, "Are you the son?"

I corrected her impression, which may have been due to failing eyesight. "No, we're married."

I was surprised at the question. When I look at my wife, I still see the lovely younger woman in our photos and in my memory. Sometimes she looks back at me and smiles. Even though she may not know who I am.

■ ■ ■

Into the Light

Preview

As a minister's daughter, Tanya Savory grew up learning that all God's children are equal and deserving of respect. But as a young woman coming to terms with her sexual identity, she wondered if that teaching applied to her.

Into the Light

Tanya Savory

One night in April when I was barely seven years old, my mother told me to put on my Sunday dress—Dad was taking the family to a church across town. None of this made sense to me. After all, it was a Thursday, it was nearly bedtime, and our church was right next door. Dad was the minister, so all we did was walk across a parking lot to get to church. Why were we going across town?

After what seemed like an endless drive, we were winding slowly through a neighborhood I'd never seen before. Suddenly we were in front of a big wooden building with no windows. Streams of people were pouring in, all of them quiet and many of them hugging or holding hands.

When our family walked into the church, many people turned to stare at us for a moment—nearly everyone in the church was black, and we were white. But then a friend of my father's, a young black minister, rushed over to greet us and led us to a pew.

Throughout that evening, the tall black woman sitting next to me turned to smile at me again and again even though there were tears in her eyes. I was amazed by her hat full of flowers and even some bird feathers, so I smiled back. No one wore hats like that in our church. I gazed at her hat until I became drowsy and drifted in and out of sleep, occasionally waking up to hear voices joined in song. Many songs were sung that night that I knew, but at the end of the service everyone joined hands and sang a slow, moving song that I'd never heard before: *We shall overcome, we shall overcome, we shall overcome some day* . . . The tall woman next to me put one arm around me and lifted the other into the air, tears streaming down her face.

It was April 4th, 1968, and Martin Luther King, Jr., had been shot and killed just five hours earlier.

When I was a senior in high school, I sat on the front porch with my dad one warm South Carolina afternoon and asked him about that night.

"Weren't you afraid?" I asked.

"Afraid? Of what?" my dad asked, giving me a kind of funny look.

"Well, you know," I said awkwardly, "afraid of the kind of white people who hate blacks. What if they had found out that we were at that service that night? Weren't you afraid of what they might think or do?"

My dad stared at me for a long moment before he answered. "Your mother and I have never been *afraid* of what bigots think of us. And we certainly weren't going to be bullied into hiding the way we felt just because some racists thought we were wrong."

"Yeah, but when everyone found out, you lost a lot of friends. Even Aunt Jo still doesn't speak to you," I pointed out.

"Not a lot of friends—a few. But that's a small price to pay to be true to yourself. I'm sorry to lose some friends, but I'd be sorrier to be living my life according to how other people think I should live it."

"Really?" I asked. "You really think that?"

"Yes. I really *know* that," my dad answered.

That night I lay awake for hours thinking about what my dad had said. I knew he was right, but I was 100% afraid to be true to myself. I was in a small town in the South in 1978, and I was afraid, very afraid, that I was someone that even open-minded people would despise. Someone who, if I *were* true to myself, would be laughed at, abandoned by my friends, and worse. Someone whose own mother and father might turn against her. I was afraid I was gay.

This was decades before gay characters on TV or in the movies had become commonplace. The words "gay marriage" would only have been heard in a punch line to a joke, and, in fact, most people still believed that homosexuality was a mental illness or a crime. In the town where I grew up, it was illegal to be gay—police used to stake out a little rundown cinderblock bar on the other side of the tracks where, supposedly, gay men gathered. It was not uncommon for the police to rough up and handcuff men they saw coming out of this bar. Then they were thrown in the jail for the night for little or no real reason. Most of the townspeople thought this was a good idea.

Every day in the halls at school, I would wonder and worry if my classmates could tell by looking at me. I pretty much looked and acted like any other seventeen-year-old girl. I passed notes in geometry, wore too much mascara, and worried about what I would wear to the prom in April. And like most of my friends, I had a boyfriend that I loved. But something had begun to creep into my consciousness about a year earlier—something like the slightest pinprick of light that had grown just a bit brighter every day until I was sure that everyone could see it like a spotlight on me: I didn't love my boyfriend, Mark, the same way I loved my best friend, Karla. I loved her more—I was *in* love with her. Midway through my senior year in high school, I became so afraid and confused about how I felt that I simply made the choice to stop being friends with Karla. The way I saw it, if I turned off the spotlight, no one would be able to see the real me.

In the darkness, it was easier to hide. I made new friends that I didn't really care too much about. I lost interest in anything that was special or unique about me, not wanting to draw attention to who I was. I went entirely overboard in my devotion to Mark, even suggesting that we get married as soon as we graduated from high school. College and my future no longer mattered to me. All that mattered was escaping the light, the fear of who I really was. It didn't matter that I was confused and miserable as long as I was hidden.

Strange as it may sound today, I was actually relieved when, one Sunday morning, I came across a short and angry article in a Christian magazine that insisted that homosexuality was a sin and that it was a choice. Apparently, all one had to do was change his or her mind about who they loved, *choose* to hate that kind of love, and everything would be okay. Supposedly it was as simple as deciding not to rob a bank or choosing not to eat too much pie. Choose heterosexuality and you get heaven. Otherwise, you get hell. I had made the right choice! In a burst of satisfaction, I decided to tell my father everything I had been through and how I had made the right decision. After all, he was a minister. Surely he'd be proud of me.

Thankfully, he was not.

"Is your decision based on who you really are or who you want people to think you are?" was my dad's first question.

I was stunned. This was not how I had expected my father to respond at all. No one I knew had ever said anything about it being okay to be gay. In fact, no one ever talked about it at all except to make fun of it. I paused for a long time before answering. Finally, I quietly said, "I'm not sure."

I don't remember what else was said, but my father hugged me. And that was a great turning point, a great source of light in my life.

Decades later, I look back on that year as a strange, murky time full of confusion about myself and about the world around me. Luckily, I had parents who, though they worried about how the world around me would treat me, did not try to change me. They never once suggested that there was anything "wrong" with me. But most of the gay people I know who grew up in that same era were not so lucky: One friend tells a story of his 75-year-old grandmother chasing him down the street with a shotgun when she found out he was gay. "She thought I'd be better off dead," he explained. "Luckily, her aim was bad." Another friend describes how her parents changed the locks on the doors, leaving a note that simply read, "Don't come back." Perhaps worst of all was a friend whose own family boycotted his funeral when he died of AIDS.

It's hard to imagine where that kind of hate comes from. What is it about love between two people of the same sex that creates such anger and hostility? Some people, like my friend's 75-year-old grandmother, have an uninformed idea of what gay people are like. They believe all the ridiculous stereotypes that they've read about or seen on TV or in the movies. The stereotypes are frightening to them—and fear is always one step away from hate. To them, gay people are a big group of creepy and weird outcasts full of prissy men who wear dresses and angry women who look like lumberjacks. In reality, of course, gay people are no different from anyone else. We work in the same jobs, eat the same foods, have the same worries, and experience the same joys and sorrows as any other human beings.

Other people, like the parents who locked their daughter out of their house, feel that it is immoral—that it is just plain wrong for two people of the same sex to fall in love. They feel that it is best to just lock it out and hope it goes away. This, in fact, was the same way many people felt about black and white people falling in love years ago. It just seemed wrong, and it made people feel uneasy. They didn't want to have to see it or think about it. So until 1948, it was against the law in the United States for interracial couples to marry. But laws designed to keep people from loving one another, and labeling something "immoral" just because it makes some people uncomfortable, are always bad ideas.

Still other people, like the family that refused to attend their own son's funeral, claim that God doesn't approve of homosexuality. Like the author of the article I had read so many years ago, they feel it's a sin. There is rarely any argument one can present that can change the minds of people who point to the Bible as their reason for disliking, even hating, gay people. But using religion to justify the way we can mistreat other people, however, is nothing new. In the past, the Bible has been used to justify slavery, segregation, and even denying women the right to vote. As the daughter of a minister, all of this seems strange to me. Like my father, I would like to think that religion is better suited to promoting love—not hate.

Luckily, attitudes are changing fast. Today, the world is far from the dark and mysterious place for a young gay person that it was when I was seventeen. It is definitely no longer considered funny or socially acceptable to make fun of gay people or tell jokes about them based on their sexual orientation. In fact, the majority of young people in the United States agree that making fun of gay people isn't cool.

And though it was pretty much unthinkable when I was growing up, now more and more states are making it legal for gay couples to marry. In only a handful of decades, gay Americans have gone from being afraid to carefully hold hands in a darkened movie theater to publicly (and legally) celebrating a wedding! That's some incredible progress. By law, marriage can no longer be defined as being only between a man and a woman. Many feel and hope that it will not be long before gay marriage is legal throughout the entire country. After all, gay marriage is already legal in more than a dozen countries, including our next-door-neighbor, Canada.

Even so, there is still plenty of progress to be made. In nineteen states, it is still perfectly legal to discriminate against a person for being gay. This means that, by law, you can fire someone, refuse to hire someone, and even deny housing to someone just because you don't approve of whom they love. These are the same states that will certainly fight against legalizing gay marriage with everything they've got. And beyond all the legalities, there are still many Americans who dislike, even hate, gay people. As was proven with the Civil Rights Movement, changing laws is easier than changing the hearts and minds of people who hate others for who they are.

Not long ago, I read a story that made me very angry. In a small town in the Midwest, an elderly woman named Sarah had just lost her partner of forty-two years, Laura, to leukemia. As Laura lay dying in the hospital, Sarah pleaded with the hospital staff to allow her to see Laura, but the staff refused. Sarah and Laura lived in one of those states where gay people can still be denied rights. Only family was allowed in the rooms of critical patients. That was the law. Laura died alone, and Sarah never got to tell her goodbye.

Within a couple days of Laura's death, Laura's only surviving relative, a nephew who hadn't seen his great-aunt in twenty years, came to claim possession of the home Sarah and Laura had shared for decades. The home was in Laura's name, so now the law said it belonged to the nephew. Additionally, the nephew was happy to be legally entitled to all of the home's possessions and all of the money in his aunt's savings. Sarah was left with nothing—no laws protected her because no laws recognized her relationship with Laura. Legally, Sarah and Laura were no more than strangers to one another. Sarah would spend her remaining years in a rundown facility for penniless elderly people.

And, legally, Sarah could even have been denied the right to attend her partner's funeral if the nephew hadn't wanted her there. However, the nephew had no interest in attending the service once he secured the deed to Laura's house.

On a cold April morning, Sarah and a handful of friends gathered at Laura's gravesite. But just as the service began, shouts were heard. Ten members of an anti-gay hate group had gathered across the road from the rural cemetery. Somehow, they had gotten wind of the fact that a gay person was about to be buried. Standing in a line and holding signs with slogans such as "Fags Burn in Hell" and "God Hates Homos," the group shouted cruel and angry comments throughout the funeral service. *Legally*, they had the right to do this.

As I read this story and looked at the pictures of the faces of those holding the signs and yelling, I felt hate. I felt like jumping in my car and driving nonstop to that little town and giving them a dose of their own darkness.

But then, near the end of the story, a comment by the elderly woman, Sarah, stopped me in my tracks. Reporters, who had crassly rushed to the scene, asked Sarah how she felt about the group picketing across the street. "Well," she had said, "I'm sorry they feel that way. But it won't do no good to hate them back."

And suddenly, Sarah's words were like a light—a light that seemed to shine all the way back to nearly forty years ago. It shone on a night in April amidst a group of mourners who chose to sing and hold hands in response to hate and violence—a group that was certainly angry and weary of being treated unfairly. And surely, somewhere during that evening, the young black minister who had led us to a seat must have reminded the congregation of Dr. King's own words: "Darkness can not drive out darkness; only light can do that. Hate can not drive out hate; only love can do that."

■ ■ ■

Acknowledgments

Gammage, Jeff. "Wonder in the Air." Originally published as "Yes, Jin Yu, There Is Wonder in the Air." From the *Philadelphia Inquirer*, December 30, 2006. Used with permission of the *Philadelphia Inquirer*. Copyright © 2013. All rights reserved.

Hamill, Pete. "The Yellow Ribbon." Copyright © 1971 by Pete Hamill. Used by permission. All rights reserved.

Hoffman, Gail. "The Blind Vet." Reprinted by permission.

Johnson, Beth. "The Love of a Dog." Reprinted by permission.

Lopez, Steve. "To Tony Lopez, with Love." From the *Los Angeles Times*, February 22, 2012. Copyright © 2012 *Los Angeles Times*. Reprinted by permission.

Mercurio, Peter. "We Found Our Son in the Subway." From the *New York Times*, February 28, 2013, © 2013 the *New York Time*. All rights reserved.

Mrosla, Sister Helen P. "All the Good Things." Originally published in *Proteus*, Spring 1991. Reprinted by permission of the author as edited and published by *Reader's Digest* in October, 1991.

Rotbart, Harley A. "Graduating to Freedom." From the *New York Times*, May 21, 2013, © 2013 the *New York Times*. All rights reserved.

Savory, Tanya. "Into the Light." Reprinted by permission.

Scottoline, Lisa. "Love." From *Why My Third Husband Will Be a Dog: The Amazing Adventures of an Ordinary Woman*, © 2009 by Lisa Scottoline. Reprinted by permission of St. Martin's Press. All rights reserved.

Scrimgeour, Andrew. "The Christmas Gift." From the *New York Times*, December 23, 2010, © 2010 the *New York Times*. All rights reserved.

Siskin, Carol. "From Shoebox to Stardom." Reprinted by permission.

St. Amant, Robert. "Promises That Bend Without Breaking." From the *New York Times*, May 8, 2014, © 2014 the *New York Times*. All rights reserved.

Tan, Amy. "The Most Hateful Words." Copyright © 2003 by Amy Tan. First appeared in *The New Yorker*. Reprinted by permission of the author and the Sandra Dijkstra Literary Agency.

Vitez, Michael. "Jack and Mark." From the *Philadelphia Inquirer*, December 22, 2012. Used with permission of the *Philadelphia Inquirer*. Copyright © 2012. All rights reserved.